The Twelve

Fishers of Men

Juel A. Fitzgerald

Juel's Creations, LLC.

Copyright © 2021

All rights reserved. No part of this publication may be reproduced, distributed or transmitted in any form or by any means, without prior written permission.

Scripture taken from the Holy Bible, New International Version®, NIV® Copyright ©1973, 1978, 1984, 2011 by Biblica, Inc.® Used by permission. All rights reserved worldwide.

Juel's Creations, LLC
P. O. Box 221172
Beachwood, OH 44122
https://juelscreations.com

Book Layout © 2016 BookDesignTemplates.com
Book Cover © 2021 designed by Andre A. Morgan, III.

Book Title/ Author Name. -- 1st ed.
ISBN: 978-1-7348583-4-1

Acknowledgements

It was not my plan to create this book of devotionals. My plan was to create a much larger book of devotionals. However, because of God's nudging two smaller books in addition to other books of devotionals will exist. Thank you, Lord, for Your direction, Your plan, and Your purpose.

Thanks to both my parents, James and Kathryn Taylor, who led me in the way I should go.

Thanks to my editor, Derek Dixon. He catches what I miss after I edit.

Thanks to Andre A. Morgan, Graphic Designer, for the creation of the book cover.

Contents

Prologue	i
Disciple One – The Betrayer	1
Disciple Two – The Taxman	5
Disciple Three – Believer or Not?	9
Disciple Four – Details! Details!	13
Disciple Five – Questions! Questions!	17
Disciple Six – Past Lives	21
Disciple Seven – What a Mystery!	23
Disciple Eight – The Less	25
Disciple Nine – Taking the Cup	29
Disciple Ten – The First	33
Disciple Eleven – The One Jesus Loved	37
Disciple Twelve – Solid as a Rock	41

Prologue

He slowly paced back and forth along the beach with both hands full of netting. The waves rose and crashed on the beach. He waded through the waters that rushed in and pulled out. Then he stopped. Like a flash, the net flew from his hands into a flat spot in the ocean. It landed; he grabbed and pulled it in. Fish flipped and flopped inside the yellow netting. He had scored with over twenty fish, each about one foot long! There was going to be some good eating tonight!

I watched this scene at the North Shore on Oahu. I saw this man, not knowing why he paced. Yet I snapped and snapped several pictures while he paced. I thanked God when one of the pictures captured the moment when he threw out the net. I could not have timed that on my own, especially when I did not know when it was coming. The first few pictures were taken because he was strategically situated in the beauty of God's creation. The latter pictures were taken because he was a fisherman.

This is a huge reminder of what God wants of us. We are to walk in search of His lost ones. We are to throw out the net of His Word and our lives as fishers of men for His sake and theirs. It is not an easy task. It takes time. It takes patience. It takes effort. It is rewarding. Unlike the captured fish, it is rewarding to the ones God captures as His own.

How much fishing are we doing?

As Jesus was walking beside the Sea of Galilee, he saw two brothers, Simon called Peter and his brother Andrew. They were casting a net into the lake, for they were fishermen. "Come, follow me," Jesus said, "and I will make you fishers of men." At once they left their nets and followed him. (Matthew 4:18-20).

God chose twelve men to follow Him. These twelve men walked away from their homes, their professions, and their families to follow Him. Those men were Matthew, John, Thaddaeus, Peter, James (son of Zebedee), Andrew, Philip, Bartholomew, Thomas, James (son of Alpheus), Simon and Judas. Through these men, lives were changed.

Disciple One

The Betrayer

> My enemies say of me in malice, 'When will he die and his name perish?' Whenever one comes to see me, he speaks falsely, while his heart gathers slander; then he goes out and spreads it abroad. All my enemies whisper together against me; they imagine the worst for me, saying, 'A vile disease has beset him; he will never get up from the place where he lies.' Even my close friend, whom I trusted, he who shared my bread, has lifted up his heel against me. (Psalm 41:5-9).

David wrote about this situation while he was on his sick bed. Jesus experienced similar interactions with Pharisees, non-believing Jews, and teachers of the law while he walked the earth. Then one of the twelve disciples, Judas, betrayed him. ". . .this is to fulfill the scripture; 'He who shares my bread has lifted up his heal against me.'" (John 13:18b).

Judas Iscariot was one of the twelve chosen by Jesus. Judas, the treasurer, was fully engaged in Jesus' mission.

> These twelve Jesus sent out with the following instructions: 'Do not go among the Gentiles or enter any town of the Samaritans. Go rather to the lost sheep of Israel. As you go, proclaim this message: 'The kingdom of heaven has come near.' Heal the sick, raise the dead, cleanse those who have leprosy, drive out demons. Freely you have received; freely give. Do not get any gold or silver or copper to take with you in your belts—no bag for the journey or extra shirt or sandals or a staff, for the worker is worth his keep. Whatever town or village you enter, search there for some worthy person and stay at their house until you leave. As you enter the home, give it your greeting. If the home is deserving, let your peace rest on it; if it is not, let your peace return to you. If anyone will not welcome you or listen to your words, leave that home or town and shake the dust off your feet.' (Matthew 10:5-14).

Judas had the same power and authority as the other eleven disciples in the ministry and was warned by Jesus about how they would be persecuted because of following Jesus' instructions. The twelve disciples were to preach only to Israel. Later a directive was made to the church to preach to all nations. (Matthew 28:18-20). Judas was there doing Jesus' will.

Yet this all changed just prior to and during the last supper.

> . . . Jesus was troubled in spirit and testified, 'Very truly I tell you, one of you is going to betray me.'
>
> His disciples stared at one another, at a loss to know which of them he meant. One of them, the disciple whom Jesus loved, was reclining next to him. Simon Peter motioned to this disciple and said, 'Ask him which one he means.'
>
> Leaning back against Jesus, he asked him, 'Lord, who is it?'
>
> Jesus answered, 'It is the one to whom I will give this piece of bread when I have dipped it in the dish.' Then, dipping the piece of bread, he gave it to Judas, the son of Simon

Iscariot. As soon as Judas took the bread, Satan entered into him.

So Jesus told him, 'What you are about to do, do quickly.' But no one at the meal understood why Jesus said this to him. Since Judas had charge of the money, some thought Jesus was telling him to buy what was needed for the festival, or to give something to the poor. As soon as Judas had taken the bread, he went out. And it was night. (John 13:21-30).

Judas had previously met with the chief priests and accepted thirty silver coins to accuse Jesus (Matthew 26:14-16). Satan entered Judas and deceived him to leave Jesus at the last supper to meet with the chief priests to arrest Jesus. Judas regretted his actions later. His remorse was deep. He committed suicide by hanging for betraying his Lord.

The Bible is a guide-book on how each of us should live, who we should interact with, how we should make disciples of all nations, and what we should and should not do. All God asks is our obedience. Yet obedience sometimes is the furthest thing from our minds. We tend do what we have determined is best for us. How can we dare betray Jesus, the One Who loves us and died for us?

Disciple Two

The Taxman

I never wanted to be an IRS Agent; I wanted to be a writer! However, I ended up behind a desk examining tax returns for a greater part of my pension-earning days. It was not a job I raved about. I did not talk about it all. Most of the time I could not talk, because something accidentally might be disclosed about where I had been. It was best not to mention it at all. It was not a job that I loved. It was a means of paying the house note and other living expenses.

Every time the minister had a sermon about Matthew or about tax collection, everyone would look at me and laugh. Who likes hanging with someone who is part of taking taxes from your income? "Don't tell her too much personal financial information, it might not go well," people would whisper behind my back or joke about to my face.

My dad called me a "Double Agent" one time and I did not like it at all! I thought he was saying I was a double agent like a spy for two different countries. He clarified it by saying I was a double agent because I was an IRS Agent and a Travel Agent. Then I cooled down and agreed. I was a double agent – one I loved, and one did not. I was two people in one!

God helped me to find purpose in a job that I strove so hard to leave so that I could be a writer, travel agent, and involved in several other endeavors. He kept me there long enough to earn a pension and retire. He turned an angry, disappointed, and bored woman into a woman who was grateful that she had a secure government job. He turned that same woman into a woman who was grateful that He picked her out from the scum of the world to become one of His disciples.

This makes me wonder what Matthew's life was like. Matthew, also known as Levi, was a tax collector or a publican. His job was to collect taxes for Herod. No one liked tax collectors. Many of them were unscrupulous. Some of them collected more than they were supposed to and pocketed the overage. Whether Matthew was like that or not is not mentioned in the Bible. Even if he was on the up-and-up, because of his job, people who were not tax collectors probably were not hanging around him. They did not want any parts of him!

Yet, "As he walked along, he saw Levi son of Alphaeus sitting at the tax collector's booth. 'Follow me,' Jesus told him, and Levi got up and followed him." (Mark 2:14). Levi became one of the twelve disciples who followed Jesus. We are not told how Levi became Matthew. It is believed that Jesus renamed him. There were occasions when Jesus found it necessary to give people new names. Matthew means "gift of God." He plucked Levi from the scum of his world and made him His disciple. Matthew's life was never the same.

Jesus used and still uses ordinary, sinful people to do spectacular things through Him. His love for everyone is the same no matter what their status in life is. He came to save the lost and free them from the bondage of sin.

> Then Levi held a great banquet for Jesus at his house, and a large crowd of tax collectors and others were eating with them. But the Pharisees and the teachers of the law who belonged to their sect complained to his disciples. 'Why do you eat and drink with tax collectors and 'sinners'?' Jesus answered them, 'It is not the healthy who need a doctor, but the sick. I have not come to call the righteous, but sinners to repentance.' (Luke 5:29-33)

How grateful are we that Jesus pulled us out of the nastiness of the world into His light? Are we like the Pharisees, self-righteous and making ourselves higher than we ought? Or are we grateful, like Matthew, by bringing others to Jesus through our hospitality?

Disciple Three

Believer or Not?

"Then Thomas (called Didymus) said to the rest of the disciples, 'Let us also go, that we may die with him.'" John 11:16.

Thomas, one of the twelve disciples of Jesus, said this when Jesus decided to go back to Judea to raise Lazarus from the dead. The disciples were concerned about whether or not it was wise to go back to a place where the Jews tried to stone Him. Thomas was the only one who boldly stated that all of them should be willing to die along with Jesus.

In the following scripture, Thomas questioned Jesus about where He was going just before He died.

> Do not let your hearts be troubled. Trust in God; trust also in me. In my Father's house are many rooms; if it were not so, I would have told you. I am going there to prepare a place for you. And if I go and prepare a place for you, I will come back and take you to be with me that you also may be where I am. You know the way to the place

where I am going.' Thomas said to him, 'Lord, we don't know where you are going, so how can we know the way?' Jesus answered, 'I am the way and the truth and the life. No one comes to the Father except through me. If you really knew me, you would know my Father as well. From now on, you do know him and have seen him.' (John 14:1-7).

Somehow, Thomas missed, forgot, or disbelieved who Jesus was even after all the time he had lived with Him! He went from "let's die with him" to "we don't know the way." It is also interesting how he used "we" and not "I". Was this because he did not want to admit he was the only disbeliever, or that there were others who wouldn't speak up?

There was disbelief among the eleven. After Jesus rose from the dead, He appeared to Mary Magdalene. She told the disciples, and they did not believe her. (Mark 16:9-12 and John 20:10-18). Jesus appeared to two believers walking on the road. They told the disciples, and they did not believe them either. (Mark 16:12-13 and Luke 24:13-35).

Later Jesus appeared to the Eleven as they were eating; he rebuked them for their lack of faith and their stubborn refusal to believe those who had seen him after he had risen. (Mark 16:14).

So why did they not believe others who were not apostles about Jesus having risen? What happened to their faith? Did they have to see him for themselves? The others who saw him first were followers of Jesus, just like they were. Could they have disbelieved because those others were beneath them and appalled that Jesus visited *them* first and not *The Twelve*?

Thomas, was the last to believe.
Now Thomas (called Didymus), one of the Twelve, was not with the disciples when Jesus came. So the other disciples told him, 'We have seen the Lord!'

But he said to them, 'Unless I see the nail marks in his hands and put my finger where the nails were, and put my hand into his side, I will not believe it.'

A week later his disciples were in the house again, and Thomas was with them. Though the doors were locked, Jesus came and stood among them and said, 'Peace be with you!' Then he said to Thomas, 'Put your finger here; see my hands. Reach out your hand and put it into my side. Stop doubting and believe.'

Thomas said to him, 'My Lord and my God!'

Then Jesus told him, 'Because you have seen me, you have believed; blessed are those who have not seen and yet have believed.' (John 20:24-29).

This is probably how he became known as "Doubting Thomas". Though others disbelieved before him, he refused to believe even though his fellow disciples told him the truth.

What will it take for us to genuinely believe that Jesus is Who He says He is, trust Him completely, and obey His commands?

Disciple Four

Details! Details!

Not much is written about Thaddaeus. He is also known as Judas, the son of James. He is not Judas Iscariot. Where he was from and what he did for a living before meeting Jesus is unknown. He is known as one of The Twelve who learned the truth of the Gospel from Jesus and was given "authority to drive out evil spirits and to heal every disease and sickness" (Matthew 10:1) like the other eleven. He, too, was sent to preach the message that the kingdom was near to all Israel. (Matthew 10:5-7). He was martyred for being obedient to Jesus in Syria.

He was listed with the Twelve with directives about their mission. Only one incident was mentioned about him. Jesus spoke these words to His disciples:

> Before long, the world will not see me anymore, but you will see me. Because I live, you also will live. On that day you will realize that I am in my Father, and you are in me, and I am in you. Whoever has my commands and obeys them, he is the one who loves me. He

who loves me will be loved by my Father, and I too will love him and show myself to him.

Then Judas (not Judas Iscariot) said, 'But Lord, why do you intend to show yourself to us and not the world?'

Jesus replied, 'If anyone loves me, he will obey my teaching. My Father will love him, and we will come to him and make our home with him. He who does not love me will not obey my teaching. These words you hear are not my own; they belong to the Father who sent me.' (John 14:19-24).

Jesus warned His disciples about the world not seeing Him anymore. He was telling them about His death and resurrection. This was one of many places in the Bible He tried to tell them He was leaving soon. The disciples never quite understood that He was leaving, why He was leaving, and what an impact His death and resurrection would have until it happened. The disciples, like many of His followers, thought He was going to be glorified as some sort of earthly ruler. It was difficult for them to understand what being a spiritual ruler meant.

Thaddaeus (Judas) questioned what He was talking about. Jesus refocused Thaddaeus' thoughts to how important it was to have and obey His commands and love Jesus.

There will always be times when Jesus tells us something He wants us to do, and we'll ask why. In those moments, He redirects us to do and not ask why.

How important is it for us to know all the details of God's plan before we obey his commands and do His will? What is it in our disobedience that keeps us from loving God? Even if He gave us all the details, would that make a difference for us? Would we really obey? Jesus knows how much we need to know. What we do not need we do not get. It is about trust, trust in God. Whatever He says to do we should do with all our heart, mind, and soul.

Disciple Five

Questions! Questions!

Philip, a Greek-named fisherman, was found by Jesus when He left for Galilee. Jesus said "Follow me." (John 1:43). He did and became one of The Twelve.

Philip then found Nathanael and said, "We have found the one Moses wrote about in the Law, and about whom the prophets also wrote—Jesus of Nazareth, the son of Joseph." (John 1:44-45)

Nathanael was not excited about what Philip had to say. He asked, "Nazareth! Can anything good come from there?" (John 1:46a).

This negative response did not stop Philip. He merely told him to "Come and see." (John 1:46b).

Nathanael discovered for himself that this guy Jesus was the One about whom prophets wrote. He also became one of the twelve disciples of Jesus. Philip did not allow Nathanael's questions to keep him from bringing his friend to Jesus. How easy it is for us to give up on family and friends by one negative comment they say about the Jesus we follow.

Jesus asked a question of Philip. "When Jesus looked up and saw a great crowd coming toward Him, he said to Philip. 'Where shall we buy bread for these people to eat?'" (John 6:5). Jesus already knew what He planned, but He wanted to test Philip.

"Philip answered him, 'Eight month wages' would not buy enough bread for each to have a bite!'" (John 6:7). Jesus knew what Philip was going to say.

Philip however needed to learn more about the power of His Lord. This was a crowd of five thousand. With five small barley loaves and two small fish, Jesus fed all of them and had bread leftovers that filled twelve baskets! How amazing that had to be for Philip as he carried one of those baskets of leftovers.

Philip is known for a question he asked Jesus. One day Jesus revealed this information to His disciples.

> I am the way and the truth and the life. No one comes to the Father except through me. If you really knew me, you would know my Father as well. From now on, you do know him and have seen him.
>
> Philip said 'Lord, show us the Father and that will be enough for us.'
>
> Jesus answered: 'Don't you know me, Philip, even after I have been among you such a long time?

Anyone who has seen me has seen the Father. How can you say, 'Show us the Father'? Don't you believe that I am in the Father, and that the Father is in me?' (John 14:6-10a).

Despite Philip's conviction about who Jesus was that led him to bring Nathanael to Jesus and seeing Jesus feed five thousand, Philip was still a little bit slow about who Jesus was. Philip did not come right out and ask Jesus what He was talking about. However, his statement questions what Jesus just said. Though hurt by this statement, Jesus gently used questions to guide Philip into a deeper relationship with Jesus and the Father.

What questions from unbelievers keeps us from sharing Jesus with them? What questions does God ask about our faith in Him that we fail to believe is possible? What truth has Jesus told us that we question?

If we have questions, we should ask them. However, let us not allow questions to prevent us from doing God's will or lose faith in Jesus.

Disciple Six

Past Lives

"Here is a true Israelite, in whom there is nothing false." (John 1:47b). Jesus said this the first time he saw Nathanael, also known as Bartholomew, approaching.

Imagine Jesus saying that same thing to us and we had never met Him before. We might respond like Nathanael did. "How do you know me?" Nathanael asked. Jesus answered, "I saw you while you were still under the fig tree before Philip called you." (John 1:48). Nathanael then immediately believed that Jesus was the Son of God, and King of Israel. (John 1:49).

Nathanael was known for his honesty. He made his opinions known. Philip brought him to Jesus. He had told Nathanael that Jesus was the one Moses and prophets had written about and was from Nazareth. "Nazareth! Can anything good come from there?" Nathanael asked. (John 1:46). Despite his disbelief something made him go with Philip to check out this Jesus.

Meeting Jesus changed his life.

Jesus said, "You believed because I told you I saw you under the fig tree. You shall see greater things than that." He then added, "I tell you the truth, you shall see heaven open, and the angels of God ascending and descending on the Son of Man." (John 1:50-51).

Nothing false was in Nathanael before he met Jesus! What a reputation! With that reputation, Jesus added the ability to drive out evil spirits, heal people of all kinds of ailments and preach that the Kingdom of heaven was near. (Matthew 10:1-9)

What was our reputation before Jesus touched our lives? What is our reputation now that He has become our Lord? No matter how good or bad our reputation is or was, God has a way of using that reputation to bring others closer to Him. That sinful wretched life of ours is used for others on the wide road to see how Jesus transforms us daily on the narrow road to heaven. Forget not what we were before Jesus found us. Allow Him to use what we were to become His light for others to see and be with Him.

Disciple Seven

What a Mystery!

Jesus said nothing about him. Not much interaction was written about him. No conversation was recorded about him. Yet he was one of The Twelve – Simon The Zealot.

Simon was not an outspoken disciple. His profession before Jesus chose him as an apostle is not known. Depending on the bible version read, he is known as Simon The Zealot or Simon the Canaanite. There is no proof as to whether he was in a Zealot party or merely zealous for Jesus.

What is known is that he is listed with the twelve apostles three times in the Bible: Matthew 10:2-4, Mark 3:16-19 and Luke 6:13-16. In these three references, he was listed second-to-last just before Judas, the betrayer. A final and fourth reference occurred when Judas, the betrayer had to be replaced in Acts 1:13. He was second-to-last in that listing too just before Judas son of James (not the betrayer).

Simon was given "authority to drive out evil spirits and to heal every disease and sickness" (Matthew 10:1). He was appointed to be an apostle among many disciples. "He appointed twelve – designating them apostles – that they might be with him and he might send them out to preach and to have authority to drive out demons." (Mark 3:14-15).

He prayed with the ten others when they had to decide who would replace Judas, the betrayer.

> So they proposed two men: Joseph called Barsabbas (also known as Justus) and Matthias. Then they prayed, 'Lord, you know everyone's heart. Show us which of these two you have chosen to take over this apostolic ministry, which Judas left to go where he belongs.' They cast lots, and the lot fell to Matthias; so he was added to the eleven apostles. (Acts 1:23-26).

Simon obediently did God's will and is listed permanently in His Word for all to see.

We do not have to be well-known or liked to be with Jesus and be used by Him. He gives us power for His purpose.

What power and commands has He given us that only Jesus and maybe a few others know about? What is our motive for doing His will? Is it to be seen or praised for a job well done? How might we strive to be like Simon, who was obedient, trusting, and spreading the message of Jesus?

Disciple Eight

The Less

A common name is given to many. Many of us know several people by the same name. It can get real confusing when several of these people are in the same room. My sister-in-law and I run into that same situation when we are together. Her name is Jewel and mine is Juel. The names are spelled different but sound the same. When our names are called, we do not always know which one they are calling. I know I have ignored the calls thinking they were calling for her, especially if it was not my husband calling.

Jesus had three people in his circle named James: James, his brother, who wrote the book of James; James, the son of Zebedee; and James, the son of Alphaeus. I wonder, when the three of them were in the same room, did they know which James was being called. Being called by Jesus probably was not a problem; they knew. It was when others called them that they likely wondered "me? or the other guy?"

James the son of Alphaeus was one of the twelve apostles chosen by God to preach the Word of God to the lost sheep of Israel about the kingdom of God being near, heal people of diseases, and drive out evil spirits. He walked with Jesus for three years, deserted Him like the other disciples did, saw Him in person after His resurrection, and continued to do God's will of spreading His Word to the world.

This James was known as James the Less. Supposedly this was to not get him confused with James, the son of Zebedee, another of The Twelve. That James was one of Jesus' top three guys.

Oddly enough in all four of the listings of the apostles and in Acts (Matthew 10:2-4, Mark 3:16-19, Luke 6:13-16, and Acts 1:13-14), he is consistently listed in the ninth position. Other than Peter (Simon), who was always listed first, and Simon the Zealot, who was listed second-to-last, some of the others shifted up or down. I am not sure if that means anything.

According to "Number in Scripture" on page 235, the number nine,

> . . . is the *last* of the digits, and thus marks the *end*; and is significant of the *conclusion* of a matter. . . *Nine* is therefore, The Number of Finality or Judgment, for judgment is committed unto Jesus as 'the Son of man' (John v. 27; Acts xvii. 31). It marks the completeness, the end and issue of all things as to man –

the judgment of man and all his works.

Just something that makes you go "Hmmm, was he listed ninth for a reason?"

James' prior occupation, hometown, characteristics, and what Jesus said about him is unknown. The Bible merely lists him as one of the chosen Twelve; that has to be enough, otherwise God would have told us more. Matthew (Levi) was also listed as being the son of Alphaeus and scholars have tried to make them brothers; but nothing in the Bible indicates they are. Just like James, there had to be more than one Alphaeus in the world. Nothing positive or negative was mentioned specifically about James the Less. He was a chosen top twelve worker for God's will and purpose. That was his fifteen minutes of fame.

Having only one spiritual talent (we all have at least one), do we often think God cannot use us in a powerful way? Do we look enviously at others who have talents galore? Do we compare ourselves to others and not God's standard in the Bible? What are we focused on, using our one talent to be pleasing in God's sight or pleasing in the eyes of others? Are we filled with gratitude for the talent God has granted to us and will do anything He asks to complete His work in us? Are we angry that He did not give us more to work with? Isn't being chosen as His disciple enough? How are we using our commonness to advance God's kingdom?

But you are a chosen people, a royal priesthood, a holy nation, a people belonging to God, that you may declare the praises of him who called you out of darkness into his wonderful light. Once you were not a people, but now you are the people of God; once you had not received mercy, but now you have received mercy. Dear friends, I urge you, as aliens and strangers in this world, to abstain from sinful desires, which war against your soul. Live such good lives among the pagans that, though they accuse you of doing wrong, they may see your good deeds and glorify God on the day he visits us. (I Peter 2:9-12).

Disciple Nine

Taking the Cup

> He saw James son of Zebedee and his brother John in a boat, preparing their nets. Without delay, he called them, and they left their father Zebedee in the boat with the hired men and followed him. (Mark 1:19-20).

What an immediate response to Jesus' call. James left his father in the middle of a normal workday to follow Jesus. Who does that? Who walks away from a lucrative family income source to follow an unknown income source? James became one of Jesus' top four apostles along with his brother John. With Jesus, James turned from being a fisherman to being a fisher of men and who Jesus called, along with his brother, "Sons of Thunder" (Mark 3:17).

As part of the top four, James witnessed many things with Jesus.

- He was with others when Jesus enabled a great catch of fish (Luke 5:1-11).
- He saw Peter's mother-in-law healed of a fever by Jesus (Mark

1:29-31; Matthew 8:14-17; Luke 4:38-41).

- He witnessed Jairus' daughter risen from the dead by Jesus (Mark 5:35-43; Matthew 9:18-19, 23-26; Luke 8:49-56).
- He fell face down in amazement when Jesus was transfigured (Matthew 17:1-13; Mark 9:2-13; Luke 9:28-36).
- He and his brother wanted to call down fire from heaven to destroy the Samaritans who had rejected Jesus (Luke 9:51-56).
- He could not keep his eyes open while Jesus prayed in Gethsemane just before Jesus was arrested (Matthew 26:37-46; Mark 14:32-42; Luke 22:39-46).

One day James' mom came to Jesus with both of her sons and asked Jesus, to allow her sons to sit to the right and left of Jesus in His kingdom. Jesus told the brothers they did not understanding what they were asking. Then He asked them "Can you drink the cup I am going to drink?" James and John said they could. Jesus said to them, "You will indeed drink from my cup, but to sit at my right or left is not for me to grant. These places belong to those for whom they have been prepared by my Father." (Matthew 20:20-23).

James was outspoken, bold, arrogant, obedient to Jesus in spreading the Gospel, and was willing to take the same cup Jesus took. King Herod arrested him and killed him with the sword. James was the first apostle to take the cup of Jesus (Acts 12:1-2).

How willing are we to leave our families and die for Jesus so that others may live with Him eternally?

Disciple Ten

The First

Andrew began with John the Baptist. One day John the Baptist was with two of his disciples. "When he saw Jesus passing by, he said, 'Look, the Lamb of God!" (John 1:36). The two disciples that were with John the Baptist, followed Jesus and spent the day with him. One of those disciples was Andrew.

After spending the day with Jesus, Andrew immediately went to his brother, Simon, and told him "We have found the Messiah". He took him to meet Jesus (John 1:41). Andrew and Simon became the first two disciples of Jesus.

When Andrew brought his brother, Simon, to Jesus, Jesus changed Simon's name to "Cephas" which means Peter. (John 1:42). Nothing is written in the Bible about Andrew's response to this name change. Andrew's name was not changed. There does not appear to be any ill feeling about his brother having a name change while Andrew's was not. Andrew's focus was on observing and doing Jesus's will – not sibling rivalry.

He was eager to bring others to Jesus.

> Now there were some Greeks among those who went to worship at the Feast. They came to Philip, who was from Bethsaida in Galilee, with a request. "Sir," they said, "we would like to see Jesus." Philip went to tell Andrew; Andrew and Philip in turn told Jesus. (John 12:20-22).

Andrew told Jesus, not another person, like Philip told him; he took the Greeks to the Source.

Once there was a huge crowd coming toward Jesus. Jesus asked Philip where they could buy some bread for the people. Philip said there was not enough money for bread for the crowd to eat. Andrew, offered a possible solution with what little he noticed: "Here is a boy with five small barley loaves and two small fish, but how far will they go among so many?" Andrew, unlike Philip, saw the impossible situation, offered what little there was, even though he too did not fully understand how it would matter. Jesus, however, took the little he had to offer and fed five thousand. (John 6:5-10.)

Andrew was all about bringing others to Jesus for their lives to be changed by His presence – his brother, the Greeks, and the boy with the loaves and fish.

How much better would our lives be if our focus was on bringing others to Jesus instead of what Jesus can do for us? Imagine, what Jesus can do with the little we offer Him in our lives.

Disciple Eleven

The One Jesus Loved

Humble, Deep Thinker, and Author are three attributes that come to mind regarding John the Apostle, one of the twelve original disciples.

All through the book of John, he never turned the readers' eyes toward himself. His writings kept the full focus on Jesus and what He went through for us. John alluded to himself when he mentioned several times about a disciple that Jesus loved. He never said, "I said", "I did" nor made any reference to himself other than as the disciple Jesus loved. He was not trying to imply that Jesus loved him more than the other eleven. He was merely saying repeatedly how much Jesus loved him. Jesus loved all His disciples and all His creation on earth. Jesus never loved anyone any deeper than another. He loves us all deeply despite our sinfulness. In the book of John, you can almost forget what author Jesus used to write this book because the limelight was on Jesus.

John was called by Jesus, along with his brother, James, the "Sons of Thunder". This nickname was probably given because of how they wanted to call down fire from heaven to terminate a Samaritan village who rejected Jesus (Luke 9:51-56). There was also another time when their mother, along with them, tried to convince Jesus to have James and John sit to his right and left in the kingdom, which angered the other ten disciples. (Matthew 20:20-28; Mark 10:35-45).

Other than these two incidents, which were jointly done with a family member, John appears to think before he acts or speaks.

- He mentioned to Jesus about a man who drove out demons in Jesus's name and how the disciples told him to stop because the man was not one of them. Jesus told them not to stop him, "No one who does a miracle in my name can in the next moment say anything bad about me, for whoever is not against us is for us." (Mark 9:38-40).
- John was the disciple known by the high priest, who enabled Peter to be in the courtyard when Jesus was arrested. (John 18:15-16).
- He was the only disciple who sat at the foot of the cross as Jesus died. (John 19:25-27).
- He was the disciple who ran fastest to the empty tomb. At the tomb, he stopped, observed, and pondered on what he saw before going in. (John 20:1-9).

Jesus used John to pen His message of love that changed John from a son of thunder to a humble author and Gospel messenger. He wrote five books: John, 1st, 2nd, and 3rd John, and Revelation. All these books show Jesus' love for us. John knew Jesus' love and makes it clear for all who have open hearts and ears to grasp this love!

How has Jesus' love changed you?

> . . .The Spirit searches all things, even the deep things of God. For who among men knows the thoughts of a man except the man's spirit within him? In the same way, no one knows the thoughts of God except the Spirit of God. We have not received the spirit of the world, but the Spirit who is from God, that we may understand what God has freely given us. This is what we speak, not in words taught us by human wisdom, but in words taught by the Spirit, expressing spiritual truths in spiritual words. (I Corinthians 2:10-13).

Disciple Twelve

Solid as a Rock

> And I tell you that you are Peter, and on this rock I will build my church, and the gates of Hades will not overcome it. I will give you the keys of the kingdom of heaven; whatever you bind on earth will be bound in heaven, and whatever you loose on earth will be loosed in heaven. (Matthew 16:18-19).

Simon was the disciple whose name was changed when He first met Jesus. "Jesus looked at him and said, 'You are Simon son of John. You will be called Cephas' (which, when translated, is Peter)." (John 1:42b). Jesus obviously had a plan for him even before Peter knew him. Cephas in Aramaic means "rock". In Greek, "petros" also means "rock". Thus "Peter" translates from that.

Peter was an unschooled fisherman. His brother Andrew is the one who met Jesus first and brought Peter to meet Jesus. The both of them were disciples of John the Baptist and had waited for the Messiah to come.

Peter was known for being extremely outspoken! This ability to speak his mind made him a natural leader. This ability to speak out also got him into a lot of trouble!

He was the one Jesus called "Satan" when Jesus told them about why He was here and what He had to suffer. Peter took Jesus aside and rebuked Him. Then Jesus said, "Get behind me, Satan! You are a stumbling block to me; you do not have in mind the things of God, but the things of men." (Matthew 16:23b).

He was the one, who told Jesus, "Master, the people are crowding and pressing against you." (Luke 8:45b). Jesus had asked who touched Him. A bleeding woman was healed by the mere touch of Jesus' garment. Peter made it sound like a stupid question to ask.

He was the one who refused to let Jesus wash his feet until Jesus explained why. (John 13:1-20)

He is the one who walked on water with Jesus, took his eyes off Jesus, then sank. (Matthew 14:22-33)

He was the one who warmed himself by the enemies' fire and denied he even knew Jesus three times. (John 18:25-27; Matthew 26:69-75; Mark 14:66-72; Luke 22:54-65)

Despite his shortcomings, Peter was the one who said Jesus was the Messiah when others called Jesus John the Baptist, Elijah, Jeremiah, or other prophets. (Mark 8:27-29; Matthew 16:13-20; Luke 9:18-20; John 6:68-69)

He was included in Jesus' top three: James, John and Peter. These three experienced what the other nine did not:

- the healing of Jairus's daughter, (Mark 5:37-43; Luke 8:51-56)
- the transfiguration (Matthew 17:1-4; Mark 9:2-6; Luke 9:28-33; 2 Peter 1:16-18)
- Jesus in the garden of Gethsemane (Matthew 26:36-46; Mark 14:33-42; Luke 22:40-46).

Peter did a ton more:

- preached.
- healed many.
- cut off the ear of Malchus.
- foretold the deaths of Ananias and Sapphira.
- rebuked Simon the sorcerer.
- met and received Paul.
- had a vision from God of clean and unclean animals.
- encouraged the preaching of the gospel to Gentiles.
- was imprisoned and wrote 1st and 2nd Peter, just to name a few.

Despite Peter's personality traits, Jesus used this unschooled impulsive fisherman to lead His church.

How are we allowing God to use us for His purpose despite ourselves?

Juel A Fitzgerald has been writing since she was a youngster. She has a bachelor's degree in English from Kent State University in Kent, Ohio.

Because of God's prompting she started blogging in 2010 and now has four active blogs. The first blog is a weekly spiritual devotional. The second is a travel blog. The third is a walking blog about raising funds for HOPE *worldwide*. The fourth is a writer's blog.

Her first book was published in June 2020, "Lives of a Gem! God's Treasured Possession". This book is an inspirational and transparent memoir about how God walked her through spiritual and physical life challenges. Her second book was published in 2021, "Bible Trek: Reading the Bible in Thirteen Weeks" takes you on her personal journey through the Bible.

She is a thirty-seven-year government retiree. During that span, she worked with the Internal Revenue Service, the Veterans Administration Hospital, and the Navy Finance Department. She is also a seventeen-year travel agent retiree. In addition, she is a five-year retired Weight Watchers Leader.

Her love of public speaking materialized due to Toastmasters. She has had numerous teaching and speaking assignments with the Boy Scouts and Girl Scouts, with the government, in the travel industry and as a Weight Watchers Leader. She has been married forty-six years, has two adult children, and two grandchildren.

Her focus is to do **all for His glory, live His schedule,** and **pray Big**!

Juel's Creations, LLC.
P. O. Box 221172
Beachwood, OH 44122
https://juelscreations.com/

www.ingramcontent.com/pod-product-compliance
Lightning Source LLC
Chambersburg PA
CBHW060412080526
44583CB00012B/545